Steam on West Country Branch Lines

Peter W. Gray

First published 1998

ISBN 0 7110 2556 8

© Peter W. Gray 1998

Publishing

Published by Ian Allan Publishing

an imprint of Ian Allan Ltd, Terminal House, Station Approach, Shepperton, Surrey TW17 8AS.
Printed by Ian Allan Printing Ltd, at its works at Coombelands in Runneymede, England.

Code: 9802/C

Front Cover: Amid banks crowded with primroses, ex-GWR 2-6-2T No 4561 hauls the 9.25am from Kingsbridge out of the Avon valley to meet the main line at Brent on 18 April 1960. This location is close to the point where the present A38 road crosses the branch trackbed.

Rear Cover: Adams Radial 4-4-2Ts Nos 30583 and 30584 double-head the 3.5pm from Lyme Regis to Axminster, approaching the summit of the line at Combpyne, on Saturday 18 June 1960.

Right: On Saturdays the mid-day short working on the Hemyock branch terminated at Culmstock. Here 0-4-2T No 1421 is ready to return to Tiverton Junction on 3 November 1962.

All uncredited photographs were taken by the author.

Introduction

Whilst compiling this selection of photographs of steam locomotives at work on the West Country branch lines, I have been aware that the term 'West Country' means different things to different people. I suspect that the further east one lives, the larger the West Country becomes. However, as a Devonian born and bred, for me it begins this side of Bristol (Temple Meads). I have, therefore, drawn an imaginary line across the southwest peninsula, roughly from Bristol to Weymouth, and endeavoured to include as many branch lines as possible from those which lie to the west of this line.

Even within this area, there were once upwards of 50 branch lines, 45 of which are here illustrated. Space, or rather the lack of it, precludes more than one or two pictures of most of the lines, though the author's personal preference for certain ones may be detected where this limitation is exceeded.

The alphabetic layout has been adopted in an effort to emphasise the varying character of these lines towards the end of the steam era. Some were by then so busy with holiday traffic during the summer that they almost qualified as extensions of the main line, while others remained quiet rural backwaters, or part of the mineral extraction industry.

The omission of the longest branch of all, the almost legendary 'Withered Arm' from Okehampton to Padstow, together with the Southern Region line to Barnstaple Junction, and the under representation of the Kingswear branch, is only because it is hoped to include these in a future volume devoted to the main lines.

A short history of each branch has been included, but little has been said of closure, again partly owing to lack of space, but also because I like to think these lines live on, in the memory and through the photographs, serving their communities in the way that their Victorian builders intended.

It saddens me when I think back to the early 1950s, when more attention to the needs of the freight customers, and promotion of the attractions of individual branch lines, might have tipped the balance in favour of one or two of them staying open. At the time I often wondered why, if the Vale of Rheidol line could be shut down during the loss-making winter months, could not the same principle have been applied to the passenger services on certain standard gauge branch lines in tourist areas? Sadly, this would have required a more flexible approach than was possible at that time, and the opportunity was missed.

However, where the then state-owned railway failed to see the opportunities, the preservation movement has fortunately stepped in to promote and successfully exploit the tourist potential of at least a few of our West Country branch lines, which would otherwise have returned to nature.

Many sections of the lines which have closed are still open for walking or cycling, so that their countryside can be enjoyed and observed in much the same way as we did, when taking these photographs in their active days. Part of the trackbed of the Kingsbridge branch, southwards from Topsham bridge, is an example of an easy country walk along the Avon valley, with the enticing prospect that Devonshire cream teas are available on the platform of Loddiswell station at the end of your walk.

My thanks are due to the authors of the many branch line histories who have diligently researched their subject and from whose published work I have constructed the 'potted' histories of each line.

For those interested in the photographic details, my pictures prior to the spring of 1959 were taken using a folding Voigtlander Vito IIa 35mm camera with a f3.5 Color-Skopar lens. In the spring of 1959 I purchased a new Agfa Super Silette 35mm camera with a high quality f2 Solagon fixed lens, which was used for most of the pictures in this book. Most of the exposures were made on Kodachrome film, Mark I at the very slow speed of ASA 10 until the end of 1961, and the somewhat faster Mark II version at ASA 25 thereafter. Until 1959, Agfa CT18 had to be used during the winter months.

Lastly, it is my pleasant duty to thank those photographer friends who have willingly assisted by plugging a few gaps in my own collection, by lending their own precious slides — Leslie Folkard, Trevor Owen and Richard Riley. Thank you, gentlemen.

Peter W. Gray
Torquay
June 1997

The Abbotsbury Branch

This trackbed was the first section of the Abbotsbury Railway, opened in November 1885. It was one of the early postwar branch line closures, and except for this short stretch down to Upwey station, which was retained another nine years for goods traffic, the line closed to all traffic in December 1952.

Below: On 17 July 1965 rebuilt Bulleid Pacific No 34088 *213 Squadron* is climbing through Upwey & Broadwey station, probably with the 3.50pm Weymouth to Waterloo service. This station had been Upwey Junction until December 1952, and in 1965 had only recently been downgraded to an unstaffed halt.

The Ashburton Branch

This line was one of several in the West Country supported by the 'Broad Gauge Interests', to thwart a perceived threat from the 'Narrow Gauge Interests' in the shape of the London & South Western Railway. In the case of the Buckfastleigh, Totnes & South Devon Railway, whose 1864 Parliamentary Act approved the connection between these towns and the SDR at the latter, the direct threat came from that most unlikely source, the as yet uncompleted Teign Valley Railway, which was proposing an extension of its narrow gauge line to Ashburton and Buckfastleigh. The TVR never received the support it anticipated from the LSWR, so when this scheme collapsed, the inhabitants of Ashburton were forced into the arms of the BT&SDR, which in 1865 obtained an Act for the extension of its broad gauge line to Ashburton. This was eventually opened in May 1872.

Following the abandonment of the broad gauge in 1892, the passenger service was mainly in the hands of one of the Class 517 0-4-2Ts, until these were replaced by the new Class 4800 0-4-2Ts during the 1930s. The daily goods train was worked from Newton Abbot, in earlier days by one of the smaller 0-6-0 saddle tanks, but during the postwar years 2-6-2T No 4405 was the regular Ashburton goods engine and remained so until it was withdrawn in 1955. Subsequently, either a straight tank Class 4500 2-6-2T or a Class 1600 0-6-0PT generally worked the daily goods train.

Left: If the church clock can be believed, 0-4-2T No 1427 (before 1946 No 4827) on a single auto-trailer is preparing to leave Ashburton with the 4.10pm to Totnes on 2 July 1957. The spare trailer rests beyond the cattle pens under the wooden overall roof, attached to the stone-built station building, the whole being of similar construction to the terminus at Moretonhampstead.   *R.C. Riley*

Right: The picturesque riverside section of the line opposite Dartington Hall has long been a favourite for photographers, and on this idyllic Spring day, 3 May 1958, 0-4-2T No 1470 was taking the 5.45pm from Ashburton to Totnes.

The Barnstaple Branch

Opened throughout in November 1873, the broad gauge Devon & Somerset Railway lived up to its name, crossing the county boundary several times between Norton Fitzwarren — where it left the Bristol & Exeter Railway's main line — and Barnstaple (Victoria Rd). With over 42 miles of line and initially only three crossing places, the B&E, which worked the line from the outset, soon asked for more crossing places to be provided.

Left: In this view of Dulverton station on 15 June 1963. 0-4-2T No 1421 is standing on the down side with the 5.15pm to Exeter, as 2-6-0 No 6372 pulls away in the distance towards Taunton with the 4.10pm from Barnstaple Junction. Standing in the station is 2-6-0 No 7304 on the 4.20pm from Taunton. Note the 'clay hood' style station barrow, doubtless necessary with the high winter rainfall on the edge of Exmoor,

and very limited shelter on the down side island platform.

Above: Still with inside steam pipes, 2-6-0 No 6372 leaves Wiveliscombe on 18 August 1962 with the summer Saturday 2.17pm from Taunton to Ilfracombe.

7

The Bodmin Branches

Left: South Molton was another of the original crossing places on the Barnstaple branch and, along with most of the other stations on the line, had its crossing loops lengthened by the GWR in 1937. It also had this long headshunt to an extensive goods yard, still quite busy on 23 July 1964, as 2-6-0 No 7306 pulls away towards Barnstaple Junction with the 4.3pm from Taunton.

This was the only occasion on which the author recalls photographing a working ex-GWR engine carrying neither a smokebox nor cabside number plate. Its identity was painted (or chalked?) on the cabside and, as No 7306 was a Severn Tunnel Junction engine at the time, I hope it was correct.

The GWR completed its three-mile line from Bodmin Road (now Parkway) to Bodmin in May 1887 and thus ended Bodmin's isolation from the main line, which had been opened by the Cornwall Railway in 1859.

Above: 2-6-2T No 4565 approaches the line summit on 23 May 1961 with the 12.20pm from Bodmin Road to Wadebridge.

Above: Bodmin had been connected to Wadebridge by the Bodmin & Wadebridge Railway since 1834, but it was the prospect of the LSWR's imminent arrival in Wadebridge via Launceston and Halwill Junction that had stirred the GWR into action in 1887. Many years later, on 23 September 1961, ex-GWR 0-6-0PT No 4694 passes Bodmin gaol on the approach to Bodmin North station with the 3.8pm from Wadebridge. This and sister engine No 4666 had replaced the ex-LSWR's Class O2 0-4-4Ts which had worked the Padstow, Wadebridge, Bodmin North line for many years, along with the occasional Class N 2-6-0 and Class T9 4-4-0.

Right: Following the arrival of the GWR at this delightful compact terminus in Bodmin, it was only another 12 months before a connection was completed down to Boscarne Junction to enable the GWR trains to run through to Wadebridge.

On 27 May 1961, after running around this train in Bodmin General station, 2-6-2T No 4552 is leaving for Wadebridge with the 12.20pm from Bodmin Road. Later in the afternoon it will return to shunt the loaded clay wagons presently in the refuge siding alongside the engine shed, before bringing up another load from Boscarne Junction and then taking the combined train down to Bodmin Road.

The Bridport Branch

Through the early 19th century Bridport expected, almost annually, to find itself on a main line from Dorchester to the west, but it was not to be, and in 1854 a local company was formed to construct the Bridport Railway, opened in November 1857, from outside the town to Maiden Newton. This line was extended down to the harbour in March 1884 and, in the hope that a holiday resort might develop, the terminus was named Bridport West Bay.

Above: Closed to passengers in 1930, the West Bay extension was visited on 7 June 1958 by a Railway Enthusiasts' Club of Farnborough special, consisting of ex-LSWR stock behind Class M7 0-4-4T No 30107.
T. B. Owen

The Brixham Branch

Right: Opening in February 1868, the two-mile line from Churston to Brixham was the personal achievement of local solicitor Richard W. Wolston. In its latter years it was normally operated by a Class 1400 0-4-2T with an auto-trailer, and No 1470 is arriving at Churston on 11 March 1960 with the 10.15am 'mixed' train from Brixham, signalled into the bay platform.

DUNSLAND CROSS

The Bude Branch

Initial construction of this line was by the Devon & Cornwall Railway, which opened to Holsworthy in January 1879, with the extension to Bude being carried out by the LSWR, opening in August 1898.

Left: Dunsland Cross was the first station beyond Halwill Junction and is seen on 5 September 1965 as Ivatt 2-6-2T No 41283 approaches with the Great Western Society special train celebrating the centenary of the Launceston branch, which it had visited earlier that day. The crumbling platform edge dates from frost damage during the severe winter weather in 1963.

The Budleigh Salterton Branch

The station at East Budleigh was opened in May 1897, with the Budleigh Salterton Railway, which ran from Tipton St Johns, on the earlier Sidmouth Railway, to Budleigh Salterton. It was not until June 1903 that the LSWR completed the extension of this line through to Exmouth, thus giving Exmouth more direct access to Waterloo via reversal at Sidmouth Junction.

Above: On 10 August 1963 Ivatt 2-6-2T No 41298 runs into East Budleigh with the Saturday 9.52am service from Exmouth to Tipton St Johns. On weekdays this train conveyed through coaches for Waterloo, but on summer Saturdays separate trains ran to Waterloo at 9.10am from Littleham and 9.30am from Exmouth.

The Callington Branch

Although not opened as a standard gauge branch line into Devon until March 1908, after construction of the magnificent Calstock viaduct across the River Tamar by the Plymouth, Devonport & South Western Junction Railway, on the Cornwall side the line had been open since 1872, as the 3ft 6in gauge East Cornwall Mineral Railway. However, this terminated with a rope-hauled incline to the riverside quay at Calstock. The incline

was closed when the PD&SWR upgraded the line to passenger standards under a 1900 Light Railway Order, and the quay was, for a while, served by a wagon lift, attached to the side of the new viaduct.

Left: The main line junction was made at Bere Alston and it is here that we see Ivatt 2-6-2T No 41302 collecting from the main line two coaches booked to go

through from Plymouth to Callington, left behind by the 12.18pm from Plymouth, which is now well on its way to Tavistock on 24 June 1961.

Above: A late evening view of Gunnislake station, also taken in 1961, as Ivatt 2-6-2T No 41203 departs for Callington, after first detaching the front two coaches and leaving them in the yard.　　　　*L. F. Folkard*

The Carbis Wharf Branch

Above: This one-mile line from Bugle on the Newquay branch, was opened by the Cornwall Minerals Railway in June 1874. It barely qualifies as a branch line, since it was 'goods only', and had no 'run round'' facilities at the end. It was always worked as a siding by propelling the wagons to the end of the line, as is indeed happening here, with this Plymouth Railway Circle brake van special on 28 April 1962 being gingerly propelled by 2-6-2Ts Nos 4564 and 5531.

The Chard Branch

Right: Ilminster station opened in September 1866 with the Bristol & Exeter Railway's broad gauge line from Creech Junction (east of Taunton) to Chard. On 10 February 1962 0-6-0PT No 3787 stands at Ilminster on the 3.12pm service from Taunton to Chard Central.

The Cheddar Valley Line

This line began life as two separate railways: the eastern end from Witham to Wells, constructed by the East Somerset Railway, reached Wells in March 1862, while the western end from Yatton was built by the Bristol & Exeter Railway and opened to Wells in April 1870. However, it was not until January 1878 that the two were joined.

Left: Leaving Shepton Mallet behind, as it climbs towards the present day Mendip Vale terminus of the new East Somerset Railway, BR Standard Class 3MT 2-6-2T No 82035 hauls the 11.12am from Yatton towards Witham on 21 July 1962. Some distance away, above the engine's bunker, can be seen the goods shed of Charlton Road station on the Somerset & Dorset line, which runs in a cutting in front of the new houses in the left background.

Above: In the Cheddar Valley bay, on the down side of Yatton station, Ivatt 2-6-2T No 41202 waits for departure time, as the 'Devonian' express hurtles through on the up main line on 4 March 1961.

The Clevedon Branch

This was another Bristol & Exeter Railway branch and was only 3½ miles long over comparatively level ground. It was opened as early as July 1847. Clevedon did not expand as did Weston-super-Mare, remaining mainly a residential rather than a holiday town. Nevertheless, the branch train was kept very busy, especially on Saturdays, when it made 32 return trips, each journey lasting only seven minutes.

Above: On Saturday 31 October 1959 0-4-2T No 1463 with modern auto-trailers Nos 233 and 227, having arrived at Yatton at 1.20pm, is already garnering passengers for the next trip out to Clevedon at 1.30pm.

The Drinnick Mill Line

The Newquay & Cornwall Junction Railway was built northwards from Burngullow, on the Cornwall Railway main line, and completed to Drinnick Mill in 1869 with broad gauge track. It was later completed through to St

Dennis Junction, on the Newquay branch, by the standard gauge Cornwall Minerals Railway in 1874.

Right: On 28 April 1962 the Plymouth Railway Circle 'Cornwall Mineral' special hauled by 2-6-2Ts Nos 5531 and 4564 has paused at Drinnick Mill Junction on its way to Burngullow, amid the clay-spoil mountains, and overhead lines radiating from the company power station nearby. Nanpean Wharf is on a short spur behind the train, but Drinnick Mill itself lies below and to our left, on a backshunt from Nanpean Wharf.

BAMPTON

The Exe Valley line

The sections of the Exe Valley line to the north and south of Tiverton were built by separate companies, the Tiverton & North Devon Railway being the first to finish, opening the northern section in August 1884, while the Exe Valley Railway completed the line south to Stoke Canon Junction, opening in May 1885.

Left: Bampton, famous for its October Exmoor Pony Fair, was the only station north of Tiverton, until the construction of the halts at Cove and Bolham in the 1920s. Some trains terminated here, and on 24 March 1962 the 2.8pm has arrived from Exeter St David's and 0-6-0PT No 3709 is running around the train. Recently transferred from Truro, this engine is still running with no proper chimney, its previous spark-arresting chimney having been removed while at Truro.

Above: Cresting the short climb northwards out of Tiverton, over the ridge separating the Lowman and Exe valleys, the driver of No 1466 closed the regulator just before I pressed the shutter. This was the train following the one opposite on 24 March 1962, the 3.22pm from Exeter St David's to Dulverton.

Above: Exe Valley line trains normally used the No 2 bay platform at Exeter St David's. On the evening of Saturday 1 June 1963, the Whitsun Bank Holiday weekend that year, successive arrivals at 6.2pm and 6.22pm, propelled by 0-4-2Ts Nos 1451 and 1421 respectively, are resting before taking families back up the valley, after their day on the beach at Exmouth or Dawlish Warren. Foreground trailer No W231W is now restored to active service at the Great Western Society's Didcot Railway Centre.

Right: Just how busy the Exe Valley line could be on an August Bank Holiday Monday is shown by this view at West Exe Halt on 5 August 1963, the line's last Bank Holiday. Despite provision of a five-coach main line set, hauled by 0-6-0PT No 3659, some of these people will find that it is 'standing room only'.

The Exmouth Branch

The Exmouth & Exeter Railway of 1855 proposed a broad gauge line to Exmouth leaving the South Devon Railway main line near Exminster. However, the imminent approach of the LSWR to Exeter, with the prospect of a far more centrally sited terminus and no need for their line to bridge the river Exe, brought about a change of plan in 1858. The line from Exmouth Junction to Exmouth opened in May 1861 and was operated by the LSWR.

Above: Exmouth station was rebuilt during the mid-1920s into a modern, well appointed terminus with two large island platforms. On 13 October 1959 Class M7 0-4-4T No 30676 pulls out of platform No 3 after placing the stock for a Budleigh Salterton and Tipton St Johns service. On the right an Exeter-bound train smokes quietly to itself in platform No 1. The whole of the area occupied by island platform Nos 3/4, including the engine shed beyond, is now a new approach road into the centre of the town. *R. C. Riley*

Right: On a peaceful Sunday evening, nearing high tide in the Exe estuary, two children stop their play at the river's edge, to watch as BR Standard Class 4 2-6-4T No 80064 drifts into Lympstone station with the 6.12pm from Exeter Central on 7 July 1963.

In the far distance can be seen the Royal Marine barracks, which now has its own halt, Lympstone Commando, while the original station now appears in the timetable as Lympstone Village.

The Falmouth Branch

Although operated as a branch line for most of its life, the Falmouth branch was originally part of the Cornwall Railway's main line from Plymouth to Falmouth. Opened in August 1863, it had taken the Cornwall Railway more than four years to complete, since joining up with the West Cornwall Railway outside Highertown tunnel, west of Truro in May 1859.

Left: Taken from above the mouth of Highertown tunnel on 11 July 1961, the train approaching on the up main line from Chacewater is the 9.12am from Newquay to Truro, hauled by 0-6-0PT No 9635. The line disappearing into the distance, on which a two-car DMU is entering the single line section beyond Penwithers Junction, is the Falmouth branch. Entering the picture from the left is 2-6-2T No 5537 with a

goods from Truro Newham depot, down by the river — the West Cornwall Railway's original terminus.

Above: The railway system in Falmouth Docks was still in full use on 21 July 1960, as Falmouth Dock & Engineering Co's No 2, built by Hawthorn Leslie in 1926, shunts a van across the road.   *R. C. Riley*

The Fowey Branch

Opening in June 1869 the Lostwithiel & Fowey Railway constructed and operated a broad gauge 'goods only' line as far as Carne Point. This was taken over by the Cornwall Minerals Railway in 1877, after this company had completed its standard gauge line to Fowey from St Blazey. Subsequently, the Lostwithiel line was closed from 1880 to 1895, when the GWR re-opened it for passengers and goods.

Left: Since relatively few passengers used the branch service, this was the view that most people had of the branch train, with its regular engine 0-4-2T No 1419. Lostwithiel station, especially on a sunny day, was the 'Cornish Riviera', with palm trees set in colourful borders lining the platform, GWR bench seats and a Brunel-influenced station building.

Above: 2-8-0T No 4273 leaves Fowey with clay empties bound for St Blazey via Pinnock tunnel, as a loaded train waits in the station loop, prior to entering the jetties on 23 September 1960. *R. C. Riley*

33

The Goonbarrow Branch

Built by the Cornwall Minerals Railway and opened in October 1893, this line served the eastern flank of the St Austell clay mining area, leaving the Newquay branch at Goonbarrow Junction and then climbing at 1 in 39 through Bugle.

Above: This branch never had a passenger service, but on 22 April 1961 the Plymouth Railway Circle ran a brake van special over the line hauled by 0-6-0PT No 1626, which is seen taking water at Stenalees, once the site of a small engine shed for the CMR locomotive *Goonbarrow*. Beyond here the line passed through Stenalees tunnel, and then down to Gunheath siding, with a reversal on down at 1 in 35 to Carbean wharf.

The Helston Branch

Right: A peaceful scene at Praze, the first station on the branch, as 2-6-2T No 4570 arrives with the 2.25pm from Gwinear Road on 11 July 1961.

Built by the Helston Railway Company and opened in May 1887, the branch was a little under nine miles long, connecting the market town of Helston with the main line at Gwinear Road.

Left: The terminus at Helston was laid out as a through station, since at the time it was anticipated the branch would later be extended to the Lizard. However, the GWR's early espousal of the 'Road Motor' prevented this and Helston remained the terminus until the line closed in November 1962. At 2.15pm on 15 July 1961, 2-6-2T No 4563 is backing off shed after taking water, before working empty stock to Gwinear Road, crossing sister engine No 4588 at Nancegollan.

Above: Earlier the same day, 2-6-2T No 4570 is seen approaching Truthall Halt with the 1.10pm from Helston.

37

The Hemyock Branch

Alternatively known as the Culm Valley line, from the river which flowed alongside for most of its 7½ miles, this was the most rural of all the many West Country branch lines. Built as a Light Railway by Arthur Pain, an enthusiastic supporter of this concept, and opened in May 1876, the construction cost was twice that anticipated and made an early disposal to the GWR in 1880 inevitable.

Above: A sample of unhurried life on the Hemyock branch, as 0-4-2T No 1462 simmers in Tiverton Junction station, while the driver chats to a passenger and the porter puts some newspapers in the van at 4.45pm on 9 June 1962.

Right: On 2 December 1961, 0-4-2T No 1451 pulls up short of the crossing gates outside Culmstock station, and waits as the guard comes forward to open them, before proceeding into the station with the 1.45pm from Tiverton Junction.

The Ilfracombe Branch

Above: The revenue from daily despatches of liquid milk to London, at first in churns and later in bulk tanks, saved the Culm Valley line from early extinction. These came from the milk factory across the road beyond the Hemyock terminus. On 3 November 1962 0-4-2T No 1421 shunts milk tanks towards the factory, alongside a full river Culm.

The Barnstaple & Ilfracombe Railway, a subsidiary of the LSWR, opened in July 1874. Nearly 15 miles long, the line crossed the River Taw on a sharply curved iron bridge in Barnstaple, and beyond Braunton climbed to 600ft with formidable gradients on either side.

Right: Nearing the summit of the climb out of Ilfracombe, most of it at 1 in 36, 'West Country' class 4-6-2 No 34107 *Blandford Forum* leads the up Saturday 'Atlantic Coast Express' on 27 July 1963 (top picture), with 'Battle of Britain' class 4-6-2 No 34072 *257 Squadron* providing banking assistance at the rear (bottom picture).

Above: Mortehoe & Woolacombe station stood at the summit of the line between Braunton and Ilfracombe. Resting after the exertion of banking the up 'Atlantic Coast Express' (previous page) 'Battle of Britain' class 4-6-2 No 34072 *257 Squadron* waits in the up platform, before returning 'light engine' to Ilfracombe.

Meanwhile 'West Country' class 4-6-2 No 34020 *Seaton*, having completed the three miles at 1 in 40 up from Braunton, can now coast down into Ilfracombe with the 6.25am 'all stations' from Yeovil on 27 July 1963. *257 Squadron* later worked out of Ilfracombe with the 2.10pm to Waterloo, which formed part of the

4.30pm from Exeter Central.

Right: A little over a year earlier, on 7 July 1962, Class N 2-6-0 No 31875 and ex-GWR 2-6-0 No 7337 are tackling the in 1 in 36 out of Ilfracombe with the 6.37pm to Taunton.

The Kingsbridge Branch

The area of South Devon centred on Kingsbridge is known as the South Hams; this is a very rural part of Devon, which until the arrival of the railway looked to the sea and coastal shipping for its contacts with the outside world. Despite obtaining its Act of Parliament in 1864, and starting work, the capital of the Kingsbridge Railway Co soon ran out, and it was not until the later Kingsbridge & Salcombe Railway Co was eventually taken over by the GWR in 1888, that a serious attempt was made to construct the long awaited line to Kingsbridge. Even so, it still took five years to complete the 12½ miles from Brent to Kingsbridge, opened in December 1893, and Salcombe had to be content with a later 'Road Motor' service.

Left: It is a beautiful early summer evening on 8 June 1961 as 2-6-2T No 4561 climbs out of the Avon valley, about half way between Avonwick and Brent, with the 5.40pm from Kingsbridge. In the final week of the winter timetable, this was the only train not booked to stop at all three intermediate stations.

Above: A morning train, probably the 11am from Kingsbridge, calls at Loddiswell in the spring of 1960. 2-6-2T No 4561 heads the train, and beyond the passengers about to board can be seen one of the two chocolate and cream liveried Camping Coaches stationed at Loddiswell. Most Kingsbridge branch passenger trains conveyed an additional van and this one has tail traffic also, possibly a vanload of shellfish landed at Salcombe.

L. F. Folkard   45

The Kingswear Branch

The South Devon Railway opened the first section of this line, as far as Torquay (later Torre station) in December 1848. The remainder was constructed by the Dartmouth & Torbay Railway Co, opening in stages, and reaching Kingswear in August 1864.

Left: Considerable quantities of general freight still moved along the branch lines during the 1950s. This is the 8.15am Class K from Hackney Yard (Newton Abbot) to Goodrington Yard pulling up the 1 in 110 out of Kingskerswell towards the Stop Board at Lawes Bridge, behind 0-6-0PT No 3796 on 10 July 1957. At the Lawes Bridge summit brakes will have to be pinned down, before starting on the 1 in 73 descent to Torre.

Above: In July 1958 high above Hollacombe beach, with a backdrop of Livermead Cliffs and Torquay, 2-6-2T No 5164 steams past Gas House Siding with a down local train. The South Western Gas Board shunter, Ruston & Hornsby four-wheel DM No 402809, seen in the foreground, replaced Peckett 0-4-0ST No 2031 in March 1957.

L. F. Folkard

47

The Launceston Branch

This line was also built by two separate companies: the South Devon & Tavistock Railway opened in June 1859 from Marsh Mills (outside Plymouth) to Tavistock, whilst the Launceston & South Devon Railway continued the line to Launceston, opening in July 1865.

Left: On 15 April 1961 2-6-2T No 4591 pulls smartly away from Lydford station with the 10.40am (SO) from Plymouth to Launceston. Lydford station, the summit of the line at 650ft above sea level, with its combined GWR/LSWR signalbox, can be seen above the train.

Above: At Launceston on 22 December 1962, the penultimate Saturday of passenger trains direct from Plymouth, passengers arriving on the 10.40am from Plymouth, brought in by 2-6-2T No 5569, are starting their steep walk up to the shops.

49

The Looe Branch

The valley section of this branch, opened in December 1860, was rather unusual, in that it was built by the Liskeard & Looe Union Canal Co, owners of the canal that it was replacing. At that time it was a purely local railway, connecting the much earlier Liskeard & Caradon Railway, which served the mines and quarries of Caradon Hill, with the ships coming into Looe. The extension from Coombe Junction to join up with the GWR at Liskeard, enabling the development of Looe as a holiday resort, was not opened until May 1901, and the GWR did not take over the working of the line until January 1909.

Above: The 8.40am Saturdays only working from Looe arrives at Liskeard behind 2-6-2T No 4585 on 2 August 1958. Despite being advertised as non-stop from Looe to Liskeard — including the reversal at Coombe Junction — it is carrying the correct Class B headcode.

After arriving at Looe on 29 September 1959 with the 11.55am from Liskeard, 2-6-2T No 4585 pulls the empty stock forward to the run-round loop situated in the goods yard, passing what must have been one of the smallest signalboxes on the system.

The Lyme Regis Branch

Left: The Axminster & Lyme Regis Light Railway opened for business in August 1903. Although the Axminster end of the line abounded in the sinuous curves of a Light Railway, between Combpyne and Lyme Regis there was one relatively straight section, which included Cannington viaduct. In contrast to the picture on the back cover of this book, which shows the 'traditional' motive power used on the line, by 1965, in a final flurry of steam activity, the Western Region had installed Ivatt 2-6-2Ts hauling auto-trailers, both quite alien to the line. The Ivatt tanks had replaced the Adams 4-4-2Ts during late 1960/1961. No 41216 is seen leaving Cannington viaduct with an afternoon train from Lyme Regis to Axminster on 27 February 1965.

The Millbay Docks Branch

Above: A busy scene at the entrance to Millbay Docks on 19 July 1956 looking across to the cranes along Glasgow Wharf. The lines around the docks were the haunt of Class '1361' 0-6-0STs of which Nos 1361 and 1363 can be seen along with a shunter's 'dummy' allocated to Plymouth Docks. The Ocean Terminal lies away to the left, while the foreground tracks are those used by trains entering or leaving the terminal.

R. C. Riley

The Minehead Branch

This was yet another line built by two separate companies. From the main line junction (later Norton Fitzwarren) to Watchet, the route was opened by the West Somerset Railway in March 1862. It was July 1874 before the Minehead Railway completed the line. Both were worked initially by the Bristol & Exeter Railway.

Left: On 24 August 1963 BR Standard Class 3 2-6-2T No 82042 pulls away from Stogumber station with the 12.7pm summer Saturday Minehead to Cardiff train.

Above: This is a location which has become much more familiar in preservation days. 2-6-2T No 4143 lifts the 2.20pm summer Saturday Minehead-Paddington service past Castle Hill near Williton on 24 August 1963.

The Moretonhampstead Branch

The single 12½-mile broad gauge line of the Moretonhampstead & South Devon Railway Co was opened in July 1866. Initially it had only one crossing station at Bovey, and a single platform station at Lustleigh; Teigngrace was added the next year, and Chudleigh Road (renamed Heathfield from 1882) opened in 1874, was the only other crossing station. Two halts were constructed later. Brimley on the out skirts of Bovey Tracey opened in 1928 and Hawkmoor in 1931, the latter between Bovey and Lustleigh.

Hawkmoor Halt bore the name of a sanitorium located about two miles distant, as the Devon lane meanders, and was presumably intended to serve this establishment. Certainly the population in its immediate vicinity was none too great, as this picture shows. Taken on 21 February 1959, one week before the last regular passenger train ran, 0-4-2T No 1466 with auto-trailer No W241W is about a quarter of a mile out of the Halt, with the 12.50pm service from Newton Abbot to Moretonhampstead.

Presumably some passengers, less hardy than those anticipated by the GWR in 1931, had complained about the long walk for which they were unprepared,because the halt was renamed Pullabrook in 1955.

On the final day of regular passenger trains to Moretonhampstead, 28 February 1959, 2-6-2T No 4117 stands taking water at the terminus, prior to working the 3.15pm departure back to Newton Abbot. Alongside can be seen the original broad gauge engine shed, last used to house an engine in 1947, and attached to it the unique lean-to signalbox.

These large Prairie tanks were not seen on the Moretonhampstead branch until the last 12 months or so, it previously having been the preserve of either the Class 1400 0-4-2Ts or the Class 4500 or 4575 2-6-2Ts.

It was a stiff climb on the final 3¾ miles from Lustleigh to Moretonhampstead at the ruling grade of 1 in 49, and 0-4-2T No 1466, which on the opposite page had managed comfortably with the single auto-trailer on the previous Saturday, had on the last day been faced with a load of three non-corridor coaches, almost every compartment with standing passengers. Consequently, No 1466 had been working very hard and the smoke from the embankment fires started almost two hours earlier can be seen in the distance.

The Newquay Branch (from Par)

The present branch line from Par to Newquay was built by the Cornwall Minerals Railway and opened for passenger traffic in June 1876, but it had much earlier origins in the tramways built by squire J. T. Treffry. Starting from a new station at the Newquay end, the new line followed the route of the earlier tramway to St. Dennis Junction, whence a new line across Goss Moor connected with the earlier tramway from Bugle to Ponts Mill. Beyond Bridges (later renamed Luxulyan) a new route was taken, through a short

tunnel and then down the Luxulyan valley to St Blazey, with a connecting line around to Par. This avoided the section of tramway crossing the Treffry viaduct and the Carmears incline down to Ponts Mill.

Left: 0-6-0PT No 4673 arrives at Luxulyan on 13 July 1961 with the 2.40pm from Par to Newquay, on the line built by the CMR. The line to the right, then cut back to the gate, was the original route of the tramway across the Treffry viaduct.

The Newquay Branch (from Chacewater)

The Newquay end of this line was also a Treffry tramway, but as a passenger railway it was built by the GWR and opened from Chacewater to Perranporth in July 1903 and through to Newquay in January 1905.

Above: On 11 July 1961 2-6-2T No 5562 is stopping at Goonbell Halt with the 11.50am from Newquay to Chacewater. Some trains ran through to Truro and one can be seen on page 30.

The North Devon & Cornwall Junction Light Railway

An imposing title for the last cross-country passenger line to be built in the West Country, connecting Halwill Junction with Torrington. At the Torrington end it took over the route of the earlier 3ft gauge Marland Light Railway, and under the guiding hand of leading Light Railway protagonist Colonel H. F. Stephens was opened as a 20½ mile standard gauge Light Railway to Halwill Junction in July 1925.

Except for the first two years, the line was worked by ex-LBSCR Class E1 'Radial' 0-6-2Ts hauling mixed trains until 1952. after which the ex-LMR Ivatt 2-6-2Ts took over.

Left: The ND&CJLR platform at Halwill Junction was separate from the main station, and at about 6.20pm on 22 August 1964, Ivatt 2-6-2T No 41249 waits on the 6.30pm to Torrington, for any connecting passengers off the 5.51pm from Okehampton to Wadebridge, hauled by Class N 2-6-0 No 31839. BR Standard Class 4 2-6-4T No 80039 will leave for Bude at 6.25pm.

Above: The last passenger train to run the full length of the line from Halwill Junction to Torrington was the Railway Correspondence & Travel Society/Plymouth Railway Circle 'Exmoor Ranger' behind Ivatt 2-6-2Ts Nos 41206 and 41291 on 27 March 1965, four weeks after this end of the line had been closed to all traffic. The train arrives at Hole for Black Torrington with a cloud of rust coming from the rail surface.

The Princetown Branch

The Princetown Railway opened in August 1883, with the trains initially terminating at Horrabridge, along the Tavistock branch. A junction station at Yelverton was not opened until two years later.

Above: Forming a vital link with the outside world in winter and visited by generations of Plymothian day trippers in the summer months, under British Railways this most scenic of branch lines never seemed to receive the publicity it deserved and was consequently an early candidate for closure. This picture of 2-6-2T No 4410 pulling away from Ingra Tor Halt was taken on 5 July 1955, in the final summer of operation, and shows the moor at its most hospitable.

R. C. Riley

The Retew Branch

Right: Built by the Cornwall Minerals Railway and opened in June 1874, this mineral branch following the Fal valley was extended to Meledor Mill in July 1912. The line was visited by the Plymouth Railway Circle 'Cornwall Mineral' special on 28 April 1962, behind 2-6-2Ts Nos 5531 and 4564, and is here seen pausing beside one of the many clay works sidings.

The St Ives Branch

This 4¼-mile line was the last branch to be constructed to Brunel's broad gauge, and was not opened until June 1877. The choice of gauge seems a little odd, since the West Cornwall main line was already 'mixed' gauge, and the GWR was at the time much concerned at the cost of eventual conversion.

On 9 September 1961 2-6-2T No 4563 rolls into Lelant station with an augmented 'B' set forming the 9.55am from St Ives.

Steam was about to end its long innings on the St Ives branch on Saturday 9 September 1961. Already one of the 1,100hp diesel-hydraulics, No D6320, had been at work on the branch that morning assisting 2-6-2T No 4566 between St Ives and St Erth with the 10-coach 9.20am through train to Paddington. Overnight No 4564 had been cleaned and prepared for the last time in the little ivy-clad stone engine shed at St. Ives, before setting out on the 8.10am to St Erth. Thereafter, 2-6-2Ts Nos 4563, 4564 and 4566 shared the passenger duties, with No 4563 later moving to the Helston branch. Almost my last picture of steam on the St Ives branch was this one as No 4564 approaches Carbis Bay along the cliff tops with the 1.50pm from St Ives.

The Seaton Branch

Eventually opened in March 1868, the building of the Seaton & Beer Railway was not without its share of the usual problems — failed contractors, shortage of capital, etc — resulting in its taking roughly a year to build each of the 4¼ miles.

Left: On 11 June 1962 ex-LSWR Class M7 0-4-4T No 30048 stands for a few minutes in the branch platform of Seaton Junction station, before pulling out into the yard to run round. Normally the Seaton branch was push-pull worked, but as it is the Whit-Monday Bank Holiday the normal train has been augmented. Opposite is the Express Dairy factory and the branch 'M7' came in useful for attaching milk tanks to the rear of main line stopping services.

Above: In this magnificent view across the River Axe and Seaton, with a back-drop of the cliffs leading out from Beer to Beer Head, Class M7 0-4-4T No 30046 is leading the usual two-coach push-pull set towards Colyton and Seaton Junction in June 1958.

As with most holiday resorts, Seaton received its share of excursion trains. For instance on August Bank Holiday Monday 1957 the Western Region scheduled two trains from the Chard branch, despite two reversals being needed on the way.

T. B. Owen/Colour-Rail

The Sidmouth Branch

The Sidmouth Railway which opened in July 1874, was blessed with a compliant contractor who completed the 8¼-mile line almost on time, though losing money on the deal.

Left: On Saturday 10 August 1963, Ivatt 2-6-2T No 41307, with the 1.45pm Exmouth to Waterloo through coaches, was halted at the Sidmouth Junction branch home signal, while I was sheltering from a torrential downpour. A member of staff took the

opportunity for a short-cut home, and as the sun re-appeared the signal arm lifted and No 41307 pulled into the station. BR Standard Class 5 4-6-0 No 73088 *Joyous Gard* took the train on to Waterloo, picking up additional coaches from Seaton at Seaton Junction.

Above: The 'East Devon Railtour' run by the Locomotive Club of Great Britain on 7 March 1965 was a repeat of one run the previous week. At Tipton St Johns Ivatt 2-6-2T No 41291 is seen backing onto

ex-GWR 0-6-0PT No 4666, which had previously been to Sidmouth and back, prior to both engines taking the combined Railtour train down to Exmouth. The locomotives left several bankside fires behind them as they climbed through the woods beyond Budleigh Salterton. Alongside the camera is Devon General No 793, Registration Number VDV 793, an AEC Reliance with 41-seat Weymann body, new in 1957, working the Ottery St Mary to Sidmouth route.

L. F. Folkard

69

The Teign Valley Line

Left: Ex-LSWR Class M7 0-4-4T No 30044 stands at Sidmouth, outside the 23 lever signalbox on 24 July 1958. The Class M7 and O2 0-4-4Ts were the regular power on this steeply graded line, before the arrival of the Ivatt and BR Standard 2-6-2Ts in the early 1950s, and later the BR Standard 2-6-4Ts.

R. C. Riley

The Teign Valley line was completed in July 1903 by the opening of the Exeter Railway from City Basin Junction, south of Exeter St Thomas station, to Christow, where it met what had been a siding extension of the much earlier Teign Valley Railway. This standard gauge line had been opened in October 1882, initially carrying passengers only between Ashton and Heathfield, since the Moretonhampstead branch was broad gauge for another 10 years. Even after the completion of the Exeter Railway, the Teign Valley line remained comparatively little used, serving local passengers and the mines and quarries along the valley, although occasionally of use as a diversionary route, when the 'Sea Wall' line was blocked.

Above: With two crowded trains crossing at Christow, this picture is hardly typical of the normal trains on this line, which had been worked mostly by single or twin auto-trailers. On the last day of regular passenger services, 7 June 1958, 2-6-2T No 5530 is southbound with the 12.45pm from Exeter St Davids, crossing 0-4-2T No 1451 on the 12.40pm from Newton Abbot.

The Tiverton Branch

Completed by the Bristol & Exeter Railway and opened in June 1848, only four years after the main line, this 4¾-mile branch from Tiverton Junction to Tiverton was the first to be opened in Devon.

Above: This picture was taken during the two month freeze which commenced the year, as 0-4-2T No 1421 drifts into Halberton Halt with the 12.25pm from Tiverton on 2 February 1963. The wind is whipping the powdery snow off the surrounding fields, while the icicles under the engine point to the sub-zero temperature.

Right: Well into its stride on the 1 in 90 to 100 climb out of Tiverton, 0-4-2T No 1471, with a well filled trailer, speeds along a freshly ballasted length with the 1.15pm to Tiverton Junction on 24 March 1962.

The Torrington Branch

Passenger trains first ran from Barnstaple (Junction) to Bideford on the broad gauge in November 1855, although the Taw Vale Railway & Dock Co had earlier operated a horse-drawn goods service as far as Fremington Quay. Mixed gauge was laid to Bideford by March 1863 and the Torrington extension opened on standard gauge in July 1872.

Above: On 26 August 1963 Ivatt 2-6-2T No 41216, with the 10.18am from Barnstaple Junction, slows on the approach to Bideford goods yard, where another Ivatt shunts. Bideford station is East-the-Water, and Bideford itself lies across the River Torridge, the road bridge being glimpsed through the goods yard.

Right: A busy scene at Torrington on 30 June 1962 with three Ivatt 2-6-2Ts in the station. No 41294 brought in the single-coach 10.52am from Halwill Junction, leaving it in the platform, and has now picked up a three-coach set to form the 12.40pm to Barnstaple Junction. No 41238 is on another set in the yard beyond, where once stood the engine shed, while No 41297 is setting off for Meeth with clay empties.

The Wenford Bridge Branch

The Bodmin & Wadebridge Railway was the first in Cornwall to be operated by steam locomotives and had opened throughout by September 1834, some 25 years before the Cornwall Railway, which later became the GWR main line. In September 1888 the GWR opened a new line from Bodmin (GWR) to Boscarne Junction, which would enable their trains to run through to Wadebridge.

Above: Working the Wenford Bridge goods on 21 June 1962, Beattie well tank No 30586 pauses at Boscarne

Junction on its return journey. The connecting line to Bodmin Road is the one disappearing to the right, while the line to Bodmin North and Wenford Bridge is hidden by the tail of the train. No 30586 was the only one of the surviving three well tanks not to be saved.

R. C. Riley

Right: At the far end of the line, Wenford Bridge goods, ex-GWR 0-6-0PT No 1369 has arrived with the Railway Correspondence & Travel Society/Plymouth Railway Circle brake van special on 27 April 1963,

which proved to be one van too long for the run-round loop. For a moment the participants fear they may have to push their train out of the loop! However, a few deft shunting movements later, the train is ready for the return journey. As a direct result of working this and later railtours, No 1369 was saved from the cutter's torch and now steams again on the South Devon Railway from Buckfastleigh.

The Yeovil Branches

The first railway to arrive in Yeovil, in October 1853, was the Bristol & Exeter Railway branch from Durston to Hendford. This was extended through the site of the as yet unbuilt Yeovil Town station to Pen Mill station in October 1856, soon after the arrival at Pen Mill of the Wilts, Somerset & Weymouth Railway. The WS&W was extended south to Dorchester and Weymouth in January 1857. These were all broad gauge lines.

The standard gauge Salisbury & Yeovil Railway arrived from the south in June 1860, its trains initially working through to Hendford, but by July 1860 the LSWR line on to Exeter was open and thereafter many

passengers arrived at Yeovil Town, opened in June 1861, on a shuttle service from Yeovil Junction station.

Left: This view is looking north with Yeovil Town to the left and Yeovil (Pen Mill) to the right. The left hand pair of tracks were originally those of the Salisbury & Yeovil, while the right hand pair were the Wilts, Somerset & Weymouth. Until October 1943 when Yeovil South Junction was opened, there had been no connection here between SR and GWR tracks. In steam days the junction was little used and on 18 July 1964 the box is switched out as ex-GWR 0-6-0PT

No 6435 propels the 3.50pm shuttle from Yeovil Town to Yeovil Junction.

Above: Yeovil Town station is seen on 30 May 1964 as 2-6-2T No 4591 leaves with the Saturdays only 12.30pm Yeovil (Pen Mill) to Taunton. At the entrance to the shed yard Class U 2-6-0 No 31802 awaits permission to leave for Yeovil Junction to work a main line service. In the station forecourt are a couple of Royal Blue coaches, which then used Yeovil Town as a staging point on their routes between London and the West Country.

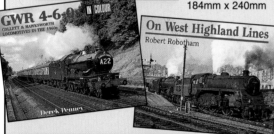